Drive Thru

The Search For
SALT

By Shalini Vallepur

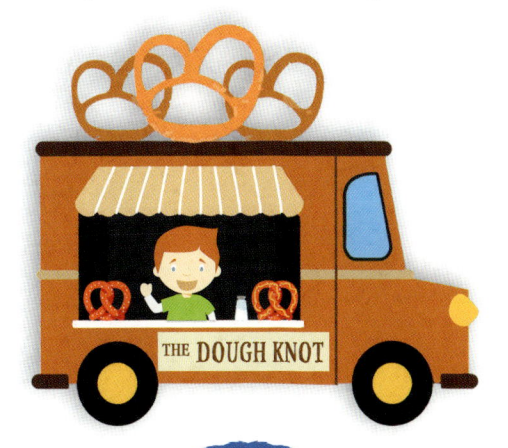

THE DOUGH KNOT

BEARPORT
PUBLISHING

Minneapolis, Minnesota

Credits

All images are courtesy of Shutterstock.com, unless otherwise specified.
With thanks to Getty Images, Thinkstock Photo and iStockphoto.

Front Cover - Michele Paccione, panotthorn phuhual, picoStudio, Spalnic, asantosg. Recurring images - Cool Vector Make, olllikeballoon, Michele Paccione, panotthorn phuhual, picoStudio, Spalnic, asantos, pikepicture. 6&7 - Dudarev Mikhail, Vladislav Gajic. 8&9 - Alewtincka, Stanislav Bokach, Antonov Maxim. 10&11 - Jess Kraft, Mc 243. 12&13 - dani daniar, Matthieu Tuffet. 14&15 - Kuttelvaserova Stuchelova, Palo_ok, Jomic. 16&17 - Svitlana Kazachek, Lucia Obregon, alefbet, Ico Maker. 18&19 - Svitlana Kazachek, Lukiyanova Natalia frenta, inewsfoto, Julia Sudnitskaya, Lifestyle discover. 20&21 - Krasula, stockfour, Gaidamashchuk. 22&23 - Radha Design.

Library of Congress Cataloging-in-Publication Data

Names: Vallepur, Shalini, author.
Title: The search for salt / by Shalini Vallepur.
Description: Fusion edition. | Minneapolis, MN : Bearport Publishing Company, [2021] | Series: Drive thru | Includes bibliographical references and index.
Identifiers: LCCN 2020010988 (print) | LCCN 2020010989 (ebook) | ISBN 9781647473242 (library binding) | ISBN 9781647473297 (paperback) | ISBN 9781647473341 (ebook)
Subjects: LCSH: Salt–Juvenile literature.
Classification: LCC TN900 .V245 2021 (print) | LCC TN900 (ebook) | DDC 664/.4–dc23
LC record available at https://lccn.loc.gov/2020010988
LC ebook record available at https://lccn.loc.gov/2020010989

© 2021 Booklife Publishing
This edition is published by arrangement with Booklife Publishing.

North American adaptations © 2021 Bearport Publishing Company. All rights reserved. No part of this publication may be reproduced in whole or in part, stored in any retrieval system, or transmitted in any form or by any means, electronic, mechanical, photocopying, recording, or otherwise, without written permission from the publisher.

For more information, write to Bearport Publishing, 5357 Penn Avenue South, Minneapolis, MN 55419. Printed in the United States of America.

CONTENTS

Hop in the Dough Knot 4
The Search for Salt 6
Where in the World? 8
Perfect Weather 10
The Brine Ponds 12
Scooping Salt 14
To the Factory 16
More Salt 18
A World of Salt 20
Pretzel Time! 22
Glossary 24
Index 24

HOP IN THE DOUGH KNOT

Welcome to my food truck, the Dough Knot! My name is Nick, and I make the tastiest **pretzels** in town. Which one would you like?

* MENU *

Salty pretzel

Cheesy pretzel

Pizza pretzel

Oh, no! I've run out of salt! I use salt to make my pretzels! I need to get more salt. Hop in the Dough Knot and come with me!

THE DOUGH KNOT

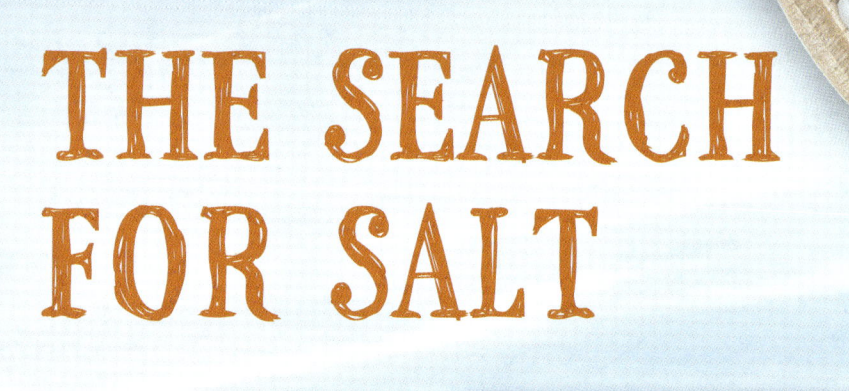

THE SEARCH FOR SALT

We get salt from brine and rocks called halite. Brine is water that has salt in it.

Halite

Halite comes from sea water and salt lakes.

Halite can be found around the world. Brine can be found in sea water and in some lakes.

WHERE IN THE WORLD?

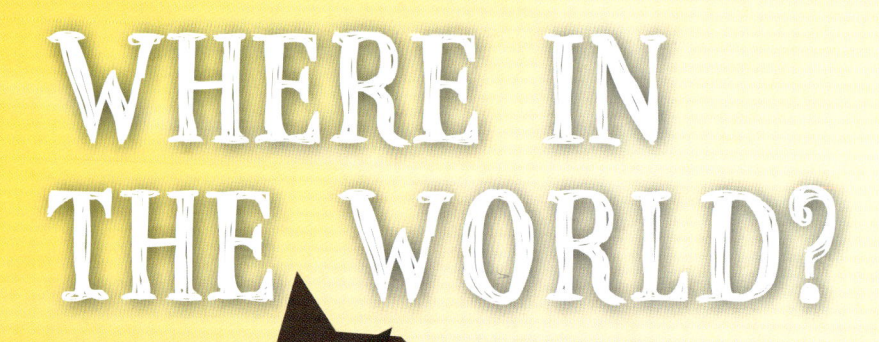

Halite is usually found underground in hot places. Big **mines** are built to bring up the salt.

Salt mine

The three biggest salt-making countries are China, the United States, and India.

The Dead Sea has a lot of salt in it.

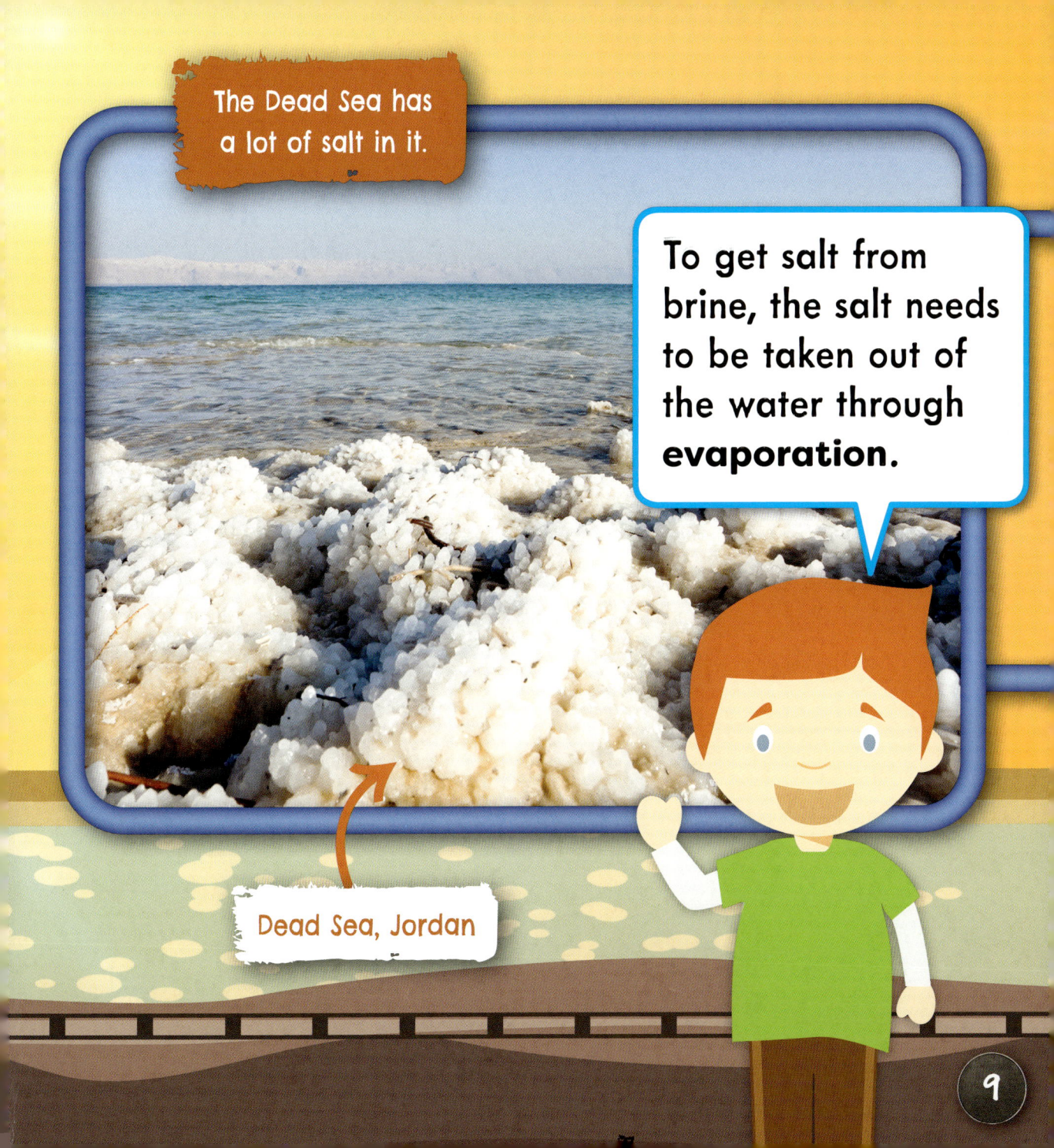

To get salt from brine, the salt needs to be taken out of the water through **evaporation**.

Dead Sea, Jordan

PERFECT WEATHER

Brine

Evaporation is when heat from the sun turns water into a **gas**. When salt water evaporates, the water becomes a **vapor**, and salt is left behind.

If salty water is in a hot, sunny place, the water will evaporate faster.

BRINE PONDS, THAILAND

THE BRINE PONDS

We made it to the brine ponds! To make salt, sea water is brought to these man-made ponds.

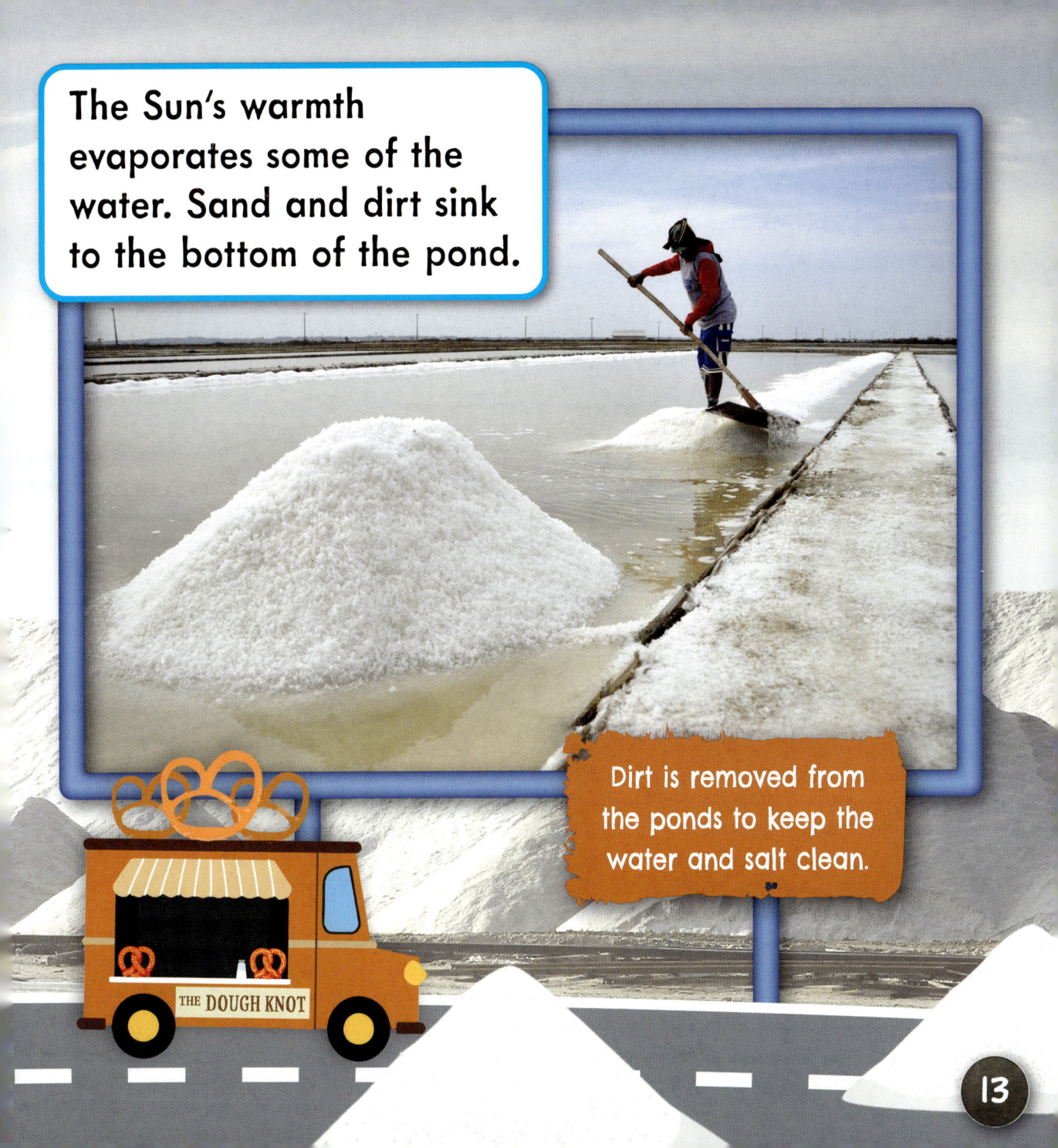

The Sun's warmth evaporates some of the water. Sand and dirt sink to the bottom of the pond.

Dirt is removed from the ponds to keep the water and salt clean.

13

SCOOPING SALT

In Thailand, it takes about four months for the water to evaporate. Salt crystals are left behind.

Workers gather the salt into piles.

SALT CRYSTALS

When all the salt is piled up, workers scoop it up and carry it away. It is then stored or taken to a factory.

Sometimes, machines are used to scoop up the salt.

TO THE FACTORY

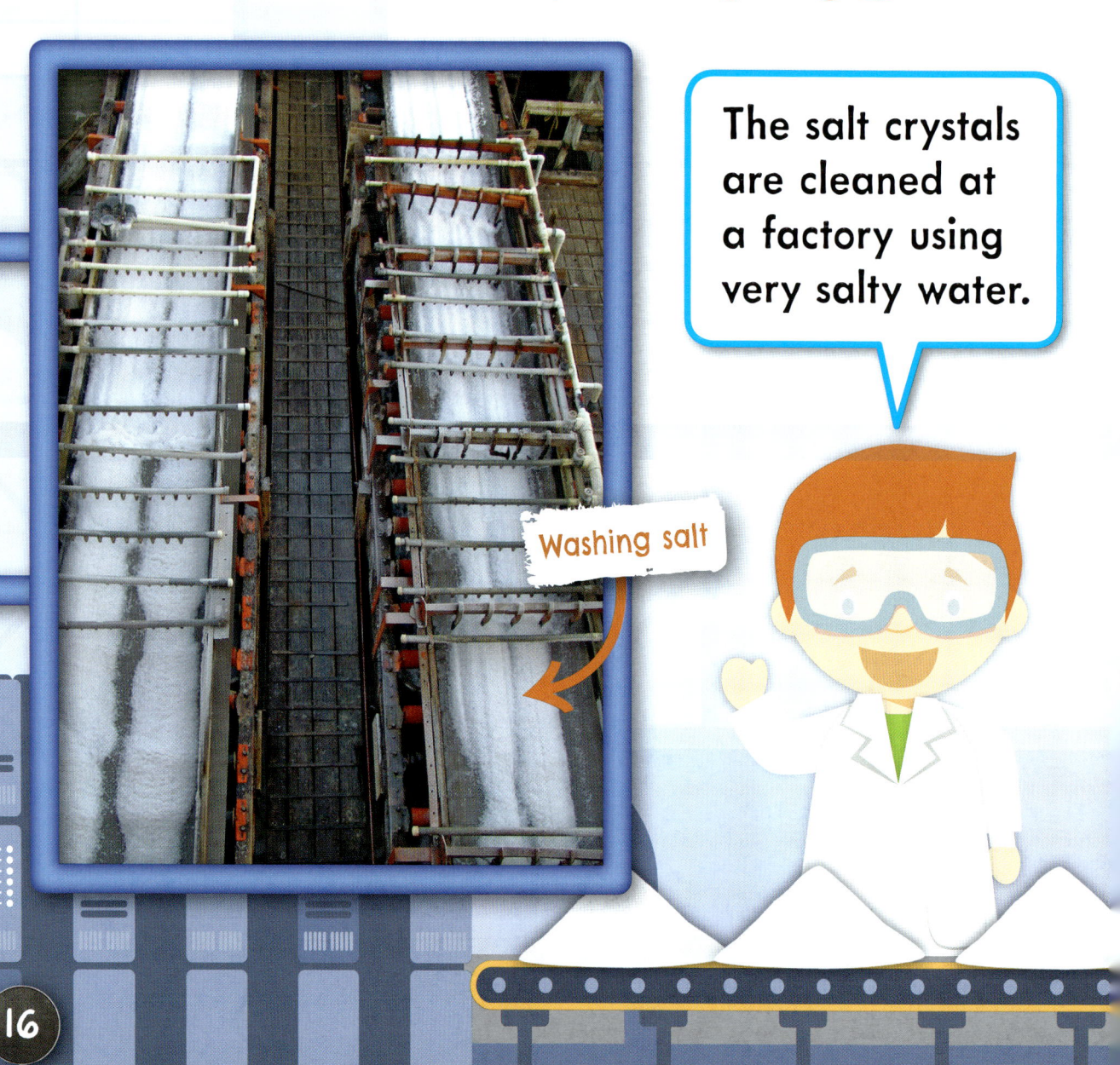

Washing salt

The salt crystals are cleaned at a factory using very salty water.

The salt crystals are then ground down to become smaller. This type of salt becomes table salt.

Salt that hasn't been ground small has more **minerals** in it.

MORE SALT

Table salt is just one type of salt. Sometimes salt crystals are not ground small. This salt is called rock salt or kosher salt.

Kosher salt

Table salt

Himalayan salt is found in mines in Pakistan. It is a type of pink rock salt. It is used in cooking, but it can also be used to make lamps!

Himalayan salt lamp

HIMALAYAN SALT

A WORLD OF SALT

Salt is very important to people. Before we had refrigerators, salt was used to kill germs on meat and fish to make the food last longer.

Rock salt is placed on roads during winter to make them less icy and slippery.

PRETZEL TIME!

I hope you enjoyed our search for salt! We made it back with enough salt for lots of pretzels. Which pretzel would you like?

THE DOUGH KNOT

* MENU *

Salty pretzel

Cheesy pretzel

Pizza pretzel

We need salt to help our muscles work the way they should. However, too much salt is bad for our bodies, so we need to make sure we eat the right amount.

Children need less than a teaspoon of salt each day. Only enjoy pretzels and other salty snacks as a special treat!

GLOSSARY

evaporation the process when a liquid such as water changes into a gas

gas a thing that is like air, which spreads out to fill any space available

minerals substances found in nature that are not plants or animals

mines deep holes or tunnels where substances such as salts or other minerals are found

pretzels snacks made from a type of hard, chewy bread, often shaped in a knot

vapor something in the form of gas

INDEX

brine 6–7, 9–12
cooking 19
factories 15–16
halite 6–8
pretzels 4–5, 22
rock salt 18–19, 21
table salt 17–18